42 MILES PRESS

Indiana University Department of English

BERMUDA FERRIS WHEEL

42 MILES PRESS
Editor, David Dodd Lee
Copyright 2022 Bryce Berkowitz. All rights reserved.
ISBN 978-1-7328511-1-5

For permission, required to reprint or broadcast more than several lines, write to:
42 Miles Press, Department of English, Indiana University South Bend
1700 Mishawaka Avenue, South Bend, IN 46615

www.42milespress.com

Interior and cover design by Austin Veldman and Sky Santiago.

Interior and cover art by Esteban del Valle.

BERMUDA FERRIS WHEEL

POEMS BY BRYCE BERKOWITZ

CONTENTS

Three...

*I know how sometimes we
stand between one self & another—
how we can become each other's shadows.*

—Maggie Anderson

One...

"Leaving Home" by Esteban del Valle

THE VIEW FROM HERE

I should begin with a few things I am:
a boy from a water-stained river town,
a photographer of tonight's evening light,
a sweet corn shoot at the end of July.

Good God: the shape of things to come
seems like a mass of grief growing
inside the Berkshire cabin my father sold.
His sister, who I've never met, wrote
on our photo, *He's not as skinny as you were.*

And then, I held you as you slept;
for whatever reason, it felt sweetly lonely.

However, I do think the best days are over,
but I saw them in my father's reaction
to seeing the housing project he grew up in
in the Bronx, on Google Street View.
How he touched my shoulder, leaning over me,
saying, *Can you go down the street with it?*

First, we went to the corner store
where he bought chocolate for a nickel
and then to his grade school, P.S. 41—
now razed and under construction—and finally
to the house that belonged to the first girl he kissed.
That one upstairs was her window.

How excited he got that where he came from was still
all those miles away, from the dock where he feeds
the fish and geese in the evenings. Beneath pink-gray clouds,
I took a photo of him with one arm wide,
twenty ripples on the water from the fish food—
some weeks don't make sense. But they know beauty.

BOULDER, COLORADO, 1989

Fuck the goose who bit me on Boulder Creek Path,
The Blob, and smushed white bread.
How wildfire smoke wafts its sallow haze and sickens the sky;
how malty brew sweetens the tongue.
There's so much potential I wish to forget.
Hobo-chalk-monikered boxcars and grip-tape-ripped kicks.
Each fingertip pressed to the moon's crisp evening
or another year's bad news. I still crave danger;
the stanchions of steer skulls and gun-shot cars,
the dragged-out years and half a truth;
hemmed-in by wind passing through trembling aspens.
This is what I know: it helps to be suffering
a mild sense of failure. And then, to disappear . . .
A purple coneflower among the common reeds.
Pink light over mountain haze.
Through luck and good fortune,
spruce, willow, and mountain ash.
That's the wonderful part about leaving,
asking and answering, *Am I enough*?
This world of ours; the strangeness of information; consumption's spiral.
But back then, there was just cocktail shrimp in a hotel restaurant,
a lemon drop store, and other beloveds.
Forget the perils of intimacy—pilot wings on a bomber jacket—
and ask yourself, what remains? And let that answer find you
inside your little boxes; while some people are loving, others are longing.

EXPLAIN YOURSELF

Last week as I was bouncing between
the nickel-gray buildings in Chicago,
drifting between L train and *el mercado*,
from bookshelf to pickled egg bar,
I found myself sitting alone in a booth at Denny's
waiting for my mother to arrive.

The familiar destination
unspools inside me—a place where,
as a child, I ordered blueberry pancakes
on Sunday morning with my parents
back when the three of us
could smile in the same room together.

So, I said yes to coffee, and
maybe to trying. My father calls
it *the right thing to do*. The waitress
set down a pair of menus, brought me
a decaf, and asked, *Do you need anything else?*
The parking lot filled and emptied.

She has a disease, the counselor said.
The side effects belong to everyone.
Here is the highway that I walked home from school on,
here is a pot of boiling water, and here are
police lights flashing on my bedroom window. And her
wrecked car beneath a loose tarp in the driveway.

At twelve years old, in the Alateen ward at St. Joe's,
I sat in a circle and listened to teenagers share their stories—
selling PlayStation games to buy hot dogs, growing
biceps from trash bags filled with bottles,
practicing math on coffee tables
next to pills scattered like loose Skittles.

In the booth at Denny's, I watched steam
rise from my coffee, and thought about
how she invited my father home,
years ago, to celebrate his birthday
and the house was empty. She never showed.
He said, *That was the last time.*

I waited for half an hour, then
set five dollars on the table and walked out,
too embarrassed to ask for a check.
That evening, our neighbor burned a brush pile,
and the dark spread into the yard, and two geese
stared at the fire, where their nest used to be.

WE'RE NOT THERE YET

Deep in the blue-green hills,
beyond the butterfly bush, hours from the heartland,
worn-down by the brocades of homesickness—a ladybug
walks along the slender leaf of an aloe plant.

Looking back now, I can see how naïve I was
in my own solitude, ankle-deep in a copper river,
among rocks rusty from chemical runoff, believing
wind through cheat grass couldn't be a blight-blown beauty.

I've tried to make West Virginia home:
the crunched-up shacks that pock the avenues,
the narrow roads that vault down hillsides like ceramic crazing;
all of it a reluctant truism, a storm that ends too soon.

But this morning, my little brother became a father.
We're only two states away, but years apart from how close we used to be.
You'll have to plant a little bamboo forest in your backyard
to relive the fort days—shooting a BB through the neighbor's window.

It wasn't until recently, in a bakery parking lot,
when a frail girl picked a pink flower from a Mimosa tree
and handed it to me, that I realized
I'm in a place of suffering.

CONCESSIONS

Sometimes I ask myself
why did I swap
the chaparral-dusted foothills,
the sun-beaten arroyos,
the secrets of bougainvillea,
the flutter of a westside breeze
blowing through blossoms
of angel's trumpets
for coal mines, for yellow boy,
for a polluted river that's flammable?
I'd love to unbutton the perfect reason,
to march with some semblance of truth
beneath branches of paw paw trees,
out of the hollers and smoky aftermath
that is now a hazy memory,
with river oak trees draped over water
that only flows in dreams,
where youth disappears
before the challenge of sobriety.
And although I forget the smell
of wisteria, buffalo grass, and taquerias,
I still wonder if my *before*
was better than my *now*. I still remember
how purple paulownia leaves
drifted to the sidewalk
in a rare rainstorm. And how
cacti and succulents
bloomed in the gardens. It's perhaps
because there are now days here
as I stare out at the foothills
that bound the state of West Virginia,
when I superimpose the foothills above Los Feliz,
and I can finally see that, through the haze
in both locations, when the sun sets,
there's a golden hour in which I forget

how I fit into this strange world,
and I get lost in the peach-smoke light
that cuts through clouds when it cuts through me.

THANK YOU, FORGIVENESS

I'll walk off remembering this:
I spent October alone, in that library
too proud to seek help; an old problem.
I slept on a couch, and you sang, sadly,
until the evening crept in. But first, winter:
we crossed a frozen highway, hand in hand.
A meditation at sunrise: *soft is my heart*.
It's always over before I'm willing to admit it.
So many times I've lost count. But to marry oneself?—that's new.
And tonight I gave my house key back.
Redbud petals bled from a branch. A nighthawk
on the windowsill. The piecemeal quality of memory.
What beauty left inside; how quietly hope blooms.

ALL THAT MATTERS

—after the eclipse, Carbondale, Illinois, August 21, 2017

Crescent moons cut   from the shade between
the breaks in the leaves,   decor on the planks
of the Adirondack chairs   on the patio floor,
where cops and surgeons gathered
in the yard   familiar strangers.

Dense bands of shadow   combed the tall grass.
Closer, unwanted advice   from a San José professor.

Before this,   minor disagreements . . .
My father and I kayak in silence,
and take endless photographs   of the sun on the water.
Everyone has their own way of doing it. That painful quiet.
Whatever we want.

At the house, totality.

And me walking away from the crowd   toward the water.
A rim of sunsets where there normally are none.
His hand finding my back. A gray-white puff of cloud
above the darker tree line. *I have to go now.*

A case of water—another way of
Come back soon. Over ten hours to think
how when the next one comes   in seven years:
What will I regret? What brief worry will sag inside?
In a crummy hotel, with his money folded in my pocket,
the quiet that I'm always chasing   settles in.

Along the night's detour   I draft him a letter
that I'll never send. This is the silent work:
slow-rolling through miles of cornfields
somewhere outside Watson or Heartville   I click on the radio.
Brake lights bleed   beneath the dusky light. The crackling voice
of a pastor,   *Another evening's cheerless blessing.*

In the morning, a fistful of daises   tattooed on a girl's hand.
The soft spray of semis passing on the interstate   through Ohio.
A funnel cloud over a pasture. Clicking on my hazards.
And I'm supposed to be happy about what?

Honeysuckle after the rain. September back east.

I suppose I am lucky
the egret's dry croak   echoed off sandstone
and my father solved the silence
with his always-yellow paddle   in our own dark lake.
Sounds like it has a sore throat. And to think

sometimes I forget to live.

IT ALWAYS DOES

The cold gray fills your window.
Red-tipped leaves dust the avenues;
the night climbs west.
The challenge of being happy.
Now you. Dry the marigolds,
hang them from a string. I never asked
who gave you the roses. Old love
has a familiar place in autumn.
Outside, the street is slick with rain.
Your lips taste sweeter now.
Candle-lit pumpkins line the stoop.
I wonder who carved them.
Where did all that sadness come from?
Soon I'll be in Illinois, where the light
grows heavy. Or maybe that's grace.
It doesn't matter. Some things
I can't even say in the dark.

JUST ONCE

I'd like to be the falling rain,
a foggy window, soft eyes,
a museum of desire, a damp yard.
My mother's hands are sweetgum leaves.
She looks for mercy in the mirror,
then disappears into the maw of night.
Why debate the subtleties?
The other day, I mistook blackbirds for roses.
The snow-dusted fields in Ohio stretched for miles,
while violet clouds drifted from Indiana into Illinois.
A silent ride home. Wreckage spreading
through rooms in a stranger's house.
We used to share problems, tip back bottles to see the stars.
Now smoke billows from the cloud factory.
Beneath a wet sky, the wind tears leaves from an oak.
And my father shuffles down the driveway,
tightening his eyes. He says, *You know,*
she wasn't always that way.

THE PERFECT TIME TO WALK OUT OF SOMEONE'S LIFE

In somewhere like West Virginia. After the bakery. Before dinner feels forced.
After a mother duck and her ducklings are threatened by a crow in a parking lot.
Over a bowl of vegetable kurma. When you're happier alone. After guilt or after ruin.
Before you count their drinks, let the sunset be the sunset.
Before you wonder where they've gone. When the mirror is just a mirror.
Before you buy that motorcycle or sleep with her friend.
Take a moment. Wait for the stars, for what *used* to be good.
Maybe it's easier to know what love isn't.

HEPBURN MANOR, LOS ANGELES

Pink bleeds into evening. The final flecks of November, a soft blue. Goodbye
jacaranda leaves rustling, sprinklers in the buffalo grass,
a busted sidewalk beneath a bay fig's shade.
I wanted you, but still I hid. On the rooftop,
beneath the sky-glow, shadowed palms swayed,
while you grew sad beneath me; the weight, a tender sore.
Brake lights pumped through Silver Lake, then disappeared into pepper trees.
In the foothills, tiny wildfires burned; over the Pacific,
planes rose and fell; the city, a jeweled motherboard.
Loneliness, its private wave. A flock of wild parrots
chattered in the neighbor's Indian Laurel, descendants from a Bel-Air brush fire,
from Pasadena's theme park. Where solitude built its current—
trips to the chandelier tree, cribbage in the hotel, the trouble with joy.
Along the dry riverbed, a methadone clinic—Skid Row now Hope Central;
I fired a revolver into a warehouse wall
on your birthday, sober. I remember angel's trumpets blooming
against that Melrose bungalow, soccer jugglers in Bellevue park,
Montana-can graffiti in the freeway heavens.
I looked at rings. I returned from Austin. I entertained my mother.
It's hard to remember every snapdragon, every peony,
every trip to the trash. For you, every hand-drawn card and candle.
My box of personal items in the corner of a shut closet.
But outside the greasy window screen, we stood in awe of the rain.
Then, a cold snap spread, the way summer ends early.

MORNING IN WEST VIRGINIA

—after Victoria Kelly

I can imagine living a whole life
in my hometown, in Illinois—
on the dock with my father,
peeling back the layers of our secrets,
until what last remains of the orange light
burns between the boughs of pines,
and the dark sky spills out of the clouds,
and we head inside to the wood stove—
this place, where, at sixteen, in a used Ford,
I jumped the hills on my way to school,
where, at twenty-one, I fired a bullet
through a gallon of milk, and my father said,
"That's what it does to someone's heart."

I can imagine how different I'd be
if I stayed behind to start each day
barefoot in the morning light,
shuffling over hardwood,
in my father's footsteps
from the bed to the coffee pot,
in a home that could've been mine
had I chosen this life that never happened.

And to think that now,
if I'd chosen differently,
that life could've carried me,
from this lonely, gray morning
in a basement apartment in West Virginia
under the coal-fire sky of autumn—
with Subarus puttering up mountain passes,
and tired students hunched beneath book bags,
walking through a doorway, as if

into a dream that hasn't yet materialized.
Meanwhile under the streetlights on the bridge,
a man, who could be my father, walks away from me,
with a boy, who is sleeping, slung on his back.

ILLINOIS BREAKDOWN

—after a note from my father, "You can't even afford to die in Illinois . . ."

But what more could I possibly want?
Late September nights, the edges of the city soften.
The symmetry of a linden tree—dim yellow
blushing out of night. Gentle morning begins.
Warehouses and body shops line Western Avenue—
a crepe myrtle in bloom. Before this,
the nature of mythmaking,
the story of silent dinner. Rain beats
through the eaves. And before you know what's good . . .
Night grows deeper. West is everywhere.
Even the sunset becomes something else—
my muzzle, a blue orchid, shivering beside the train track.
The song is still in my head. I'd rather fucking live.

Two...

"Feral Child" by Esteban del Valle

APPLE ORCHARD ROAD

—after Edward Hirsch

I remember my father sprinkling cinder on black ice,
the deer eating persimmons in the valley,
thousands of stars between the branches of my mother's fingers.
For years I've walked away, the old me
on the railroad tracks, behind bars with buckling walls,
where neon lights illuminate pink clouds of cigarette smoke,
but now I've returned to the moon's cracked beam.
I've come to stand before the wooden shacks
along the tin-colored highway, where nothing has changed,
& nothing remains of youth either.
I've come to walk barefoot through icy leaves.
I've come to listen to the screen door bang,
to feel my mother's frail hand grip my wrist,
until she slurs her words to match the best of worst memories,
words that burn like sour mash against the throat,
saying, *Honey, you're just like me.*

SIXTH GRADE AUTOBIOGRAPHY

—after Donika Ross Kelly

We live in Carbondale, Illinois.
We have a wood stove, a TV antenna, and a deer head hanging on the wall.
Mom decorates it with Christmas lights, a Santa hat, and calls it Rudolph.
My favorite things are secrets, sugar-strawberries,
and pretending chopped logs are bazookas. I pick green beans in the garden
and play basketball with Dad at sunset.
He runs marathons, and at the finish line we wrap him with aluminum foil.
He says he feels like Superman, and sometimes leftovers.
He hugs me and I feel old in his arms. I'm afraid of the dark,
being separated on vacation during a storm, and liars.
Hurricane Erin splits our Gulf Shores' rental with a billboard;
we lay on cots in a gymnasium turned Red Cross shelter.
Burger King serves free breakfast sandwiches to displaced families.
Sleeping alone is nearly impossible.
Our dog, Digit, banana-white and curly-haired, tugs on the blankets
at midnight. I believe in ghosts.
I have three half-sisters and one half-brother
and the most RBI's in little league.
Girls say I look like Yeah Yeah from *The Sandlot*.
We have a crab apple tree. A rose bush. And three maple trees.
I run through falling helicopter seeds, and cumulus clouds are my favorite.
I lie in the grass, and decide what animal I'd be: a duck.
July Fourth sleepovers. All of us drunk
on stolen cigarettes, chlorine kisses, and being out in the yard after 10 p.m.
Marco Polo and Coors Light cans. Buffalo Springfield and Warren G.
Sometimes Mom dancing with Dad.
Sometimes me dancing with the dog. Even though he bites,
I'm sure that he loves me. Whenever we pause,
he cocks his head, and then howls with his whole body.

HOW THE JOURNEY WORKED

We drove to the Elk's on Shoemaker.
We scouted and established a drill—in case of rain,
in case of ruin. *Call, then go. I'll find you here.*
Here are the aisles in Farm Fresh Milk,
the smell of blood and honey,
a half-gallon of chocolate, capped in glass;
each footfall illuminates suffering.
There's pleasure in peeled plastic, in scratched polymer.
We buy lottery tickets, because there are Mondays.
I recount each thunderstorm; I meditate. Some days,
I'm by the hospital where you opened like an orange
and I feel time grow buoyant then dissolve like a pill.
It's impossible to forget December,
driving to Chicago with you. That camper tipped on its side,
the walls busted out from within, the drag marks on the ice.
I love to say, *My father, My father is . . .*
But when I picture that wreck on I-57,
I picture a warm soda can leaking in the yellow grass
after a bullet has passed through:
the splintered metal fingers, lithe and shivering,
in the wind, in the field.
Fifty yards away, a loose mattress, bare and sheetless,
ejected from its room onto the highway's snowy shoulder.
How some families end with a little privacy; others with a boom.
I ate my cereal. I drank my soda. My father's been sober twenty years.
Thunderstorms are nothing compared to that.
Escape routes are nothing. Each moment is
stepping off a building; to be alive twice.

WHAT REMAINS

—after the Permanent Exhibition, U.S. Holocaust Memorial Museum, D.C.

In the dream, I'm ten and my father brings home a battered suitcase
          from a business trip to Berlin, Vienna, Chicago—I don't know.
I could've done a lot differently, but didn't.
He takes me into the woods and shows me how to fire a gun.
Imagine everything that angers you on the other end of that bullet.
When the clip is empty, the gunpowder cloud swells between us.
What's the word for you'll be better off without me?
A song hollowed by night, the wind tears through the maples.
His hands are my hands; our veins are Israel.
          In the damp earth, we dig a hole.

PLEASANT HILL MOBILE HOME PARK

If I told you the wind whistles the prairie's violent ballad,
      would you believe this world is a decent place?

1996: *Hoop Dreams*-twilight, microwaved hoagies (a.k.a. making dinner),
      and browsing conviction reports in Dad's parolee binder.

Tall Paul next door in the Airstream.
He wore a do-rag, blue jean overalls, and stood at the bus stop beside the llama farm.
He looked like a drifter in an old movie.

I'd bat whiffle balls and acorns from our driveway onto the rooftops of other trailers.
One time, our neighbor rushed outside because he thought it was hailing.

The same neighbor bought his girlfriend a Pontiac Fiero, which he later called a
    lemon.
I didn't understand it
but I remember feeling like the world was bigger than I knew.

One afternoon Chris and I walked off into a field of big bluestem . . .

We found a burned-out trailer. The door hung open like a slack mouth.
No steps. The floor up to our chests.

Swastikas and KKK written in drippy white spray paint on the charred cabinets.
I didn't know what the symbols meant,
but I felt a tingling in my gut looking at them.

Pick a giant foxtail, pop the stem in your mouth, and smile. Wait for dark.

AND NOW FOR THE INTERACTIVE PORTION OF THE EVENING

Moss-colored corduroys, bleached orange hair,
a Nirvana Smiley Face t-shirt.
Elbows embedded with busted bits of green glass.
Calling out, *The world's so fucked* until
You don't need my permission to express yourself.
I'm in the low-rise projects before birthday with Mom.
Fifteen years since I stepped inside her house.
Easier to say than believe. Under blood moon,
Illinois Central Gulf glows glacier-blue,
blown by prairie wind.
In the mind, rusty shotgun holes in church doors
are warm, too. What's missing?
Bald Cypress trees, the smell of blacktop,
and a purple Powell blank.
I'm always writing a letter to life's unnamable moments.
How my brother, Evan, cooled the hollows left inside.
The doors I've forgotten to close;
unmoored or unmothered youth. Still,
I miss your pork chops, your sing-songy *I love yous*,
how unhappy you looked through a window.
I'm sorry for pushing my jaw out; the cruelty's clean unsettling.
In February, the sun came out. I'm working on forgiveness.
The bright light through the window,
what subtle healing I search for.
Not unlike the shrapnel marks,
the blight, the door on Cedar Creek.
I have these shoulder scars to show you.
I have your chin scar in here. I hated how much you drank,
and how much I did too. What it means to exist
in this world? Another list. Another week.

AND SOMETIMES STILL, OTHERS I THINK

I see the bamboo forest,
the unlit fire pit, the blue plastic kiddie pool,
and Evan's crimson hoodie after I fired a BB through it.

Later, removing the window screen at Hepburn Manor,
rinsing it in the tub. The smog grease
draining away. Something inside. The shape of loss.

Skateboarding beneath the brutalist breezeway
with lost students and memory; between the old and new.
Maybe it's only home in hindsight.

Now, I am here. In a dull-lit basement,
remembering the brown sectional, Nerf gun wars, and a cat named Pizza.
How one travels with such darkness; how infrequent real love is.

When summer washed away, a warm little wisdom brightened inside.
Lucky me; a pumpkin tree. I'd say we, but this now
is the way it all makes sense: *I'll answer this when I see you.*

YEAH, SURE

I thought about ending it, and shame followed that—
I'd like to say age helped, but that would be dismissive
            to the rust-hued maple, rain tapping the yard.

It took so many years; and *boy they came*:
            red apples, small griefs.
A pumpkin's shadow crosses the cedar-wood chest.

Downtown Chicago, through this tilted rock's glass.
I'm thinking about Marsha—that's my mother.
On a quiet bench, emptied of thought, the sky is a wash

            of bright pink leaves and clouds torn to vapor.
Lake Michigan checkered with boxes of buttery light.
Tonight's confetti fuzzy on the dark, greasy water.

Maybe this is San Francisco and the life we could've had,
            the one I still dream of
or maybe it's a rope hanging from a tree in the front yard.

I'm done with what *could've been*. Something chipped inside,
long ago; another spoiled piece of fruit, yet here I am. A young man
wishing I still pressed piano keys. Look at the white peonies.

I suppose this is another kind of song. I mean the falling leaves
            or when I hear your name.
All of this is just to say, *Here comes the wind—*

SUNNYSIDE AND CLAREMONT, CHICAGO

Tonight, the Queen of Angels holds still—
a rain-washed sidewalk swept of worry—
and all my wants are captured in the blurred window of a passing train.

I never told you how afraid I was.
The things we assume others know—
the secret graphs of reason.
The memories withheld in the face of leaves
flutter like flakes of garlic-skin on a highway,
a portal away from regret . . .

Back on Montrose, stepping through wet petals,
between my fingers, the history of wind through green ash,
the mystery of a stranger's sigh . . .

Whatever it is that he can't give you, can you live without it?

At home in a dark bar,
another hospital haunted by cravings,
I wait for you.
The door is always open,
though closure has yet to arrive.

AFTER YOU ALMOST DIVORCED YOUR HUSBAND

I've heard *it's complicated* before.
To leave & to stay are two entirely different hells.

The facetious strand of hair on the pillow.
Repulsed by the anger of *it's not enough*.

Instead you sleep less, eat less,
          glass clinks in the trash, in the sink . . .

Cicadas screech through the screen's teeth.

Lying next to this one now
you kiss the possibilities
& run your hands down all your fantasies,
          complete with expiration dates.

So, this is what casual looks like?
A pie graph: mostly disappointment,
          some lack of experience, the rest—time filled, time not.

And then comes feeling special,
          painting angels on the back of your eyelids.

And then comes reality,
          thoughts of getting a dog.

And then comes clarity,
the *I'm fine now* blooming within.

SUMMERTIME CHI

From a rooftop on Lincoln Avenue
       the fountain fills with angel wings.
Summer's humid cape trails
       your bike through grid-patterned streets.

Windblown, lake effect, rain-washed leaves.
       Jazz music means: Uptown, red line.
Train window. I believe
       this city belongs to me, and Capone
still ghost-tags rooftop burners.

I love the hijacked look of a girl
       on the train as she loses her balance,
and reaches for the bar. This is how
       you learn to love again.

In Chicago, blue hue on sun brick.
       Flashlight beams rope through dark apartments,
a police cruiser jumps the curb.
       You might overhear: "I marched
with Zombies last night."

From the L, watch it zip by:
       fixie in Logan Square,
jungle smoke-stained avenues,
       the spirt of Nelson Algren,
the spirit of the stockyard,
       transplants emerging from tunnels.
You can find your way in the summertime.

Then, I see my own breath
       while stumbling down the sidewalk beside you.
On a cool night, we catch a cab,
       because the bus is blocks away.

Tomorrow we'll ride the rails
       and the sun will crest over the lake
and the body count will grow
       and glow like neon in the rain.

WE DON'T TAKE BREAKS, WE JUST BREAK

I learned a lot from drinking,
        more from not.
I dreamed that I was a drifter,
        the night stabbed with stars.
I'm not an alcoholic. I was
        and that's exactly how I'd start again.

I don't even like camping.
I sleep with a box fan running
        and read by lamplight.

Through a screen caked with smog-grease,
        morning begins.
Valley oak leaves scuttle; a memory
        cramps in the skull.
My boss called me
        an "Orchid Killer"
        when I overwatered his plant.
"Get the fuck out of my office!"
There's no *gardener* on my résumé.
I poured a little then. I pour a little now.
The ice in my gin melts.

An old photograph arrived in the mail:
        A drifter and me on a sidewalk.
Him, wearing shopping bags on his feet.
He passed his bottle. Beneath the surface
I wished my fingerprints could whistle.
"Isn't that lonely?" someone said.

THE GOOD LIFE

Audio-texting script ideas past Korean BBQ joints
         as if I was somebody who might matter soon.
In a police-auction-bought Chevy, hundred and fifty dollar suit—
not tailored—a tie—ironed, not pressed—miserable, yet *trying*.
more interested in graffiti on billboards than awards ceremonies,
in King on Crenshaw and Wilshire than box-office Mondays,
in Biggie at the red light of Wilshire and Fairfax
         than in a *2001 Space Odyssey* exhibit at LACMA.
When I was sixteen I spotted a GKAE bomb off the freeway.
And still Black BMWs zip west. The gold now faded, razed.
The voices, earpieces, trapped in bumper-to-bumper bravado.
What prayers arrive on payday get swallowed into the Pacific by nightfall;
sipping *La Palomas* by the pool, more like night runs for Froyo.
Later, a kid kickflips the twelve-set at Hollywood High.
And I'm getting my teeth pulled, thinking sobriety might make me happy.
We all know Napa is beautiful in May and talent doesn't always matter.
The one-year grind of an assistant—what it takes to make it;
that industry standard—*assumption is the mother of all fuck-ups*.
One time, flying into LAX, I spotted Saber's roller in the dry river.
Later, at dusk, as purple light slid behind a row of Italian cypress trees,
their pointed tops like little gnome hats, I undid my tie and tossed it
like a bottle off my roof, into the traffic on Hoover and Hyperion.
A river of brake lights aglow along the 101, through East Hollywood,
while a helicopter beam swept through Bellevue Park.
And I felt how my father must've felt, the day I drove west.

THE MOTORCYCLE I'LL NEVER HAVE

—after the 1933 Indian Four

Black, Model 403—golden age of the fours.
Foot clutching on a fire road, hand-shifting on a cow trail,
the switch to left so police could draw and shoot—
that old throttle myth—and tobacco can covers.
First, it was Henderson. Then, Ace. Later,
Stephanie nicknamed me B.A. We haven't spoken in years.
Sacramento and all the sadness on a gold tower bridge.
On a sprung saddle, the low-end torque, the depression.
What wide fans, what spiked debt—what money not left.
But to dream of the tell-tale speedometer's red needle,
the mercy of a little twisted pavement.
To *enjoy the ride* through Bear Tooth Pass,
up the Pig Trail Byway on leaf tour;
another kaleidoscope in wait; 30 horses
running beneath a hard-tail on Sunday afternoon.
Another *if only*: a trip to Israel with my father.
But all this dreaming for what? A luxury few can afford.
Ideally, I'll be in Chicago on a late fall evening,
when the shallow sidewalk puddles fill with elm leaves
and the L knock-rattles between alleys of two and three flats,
the narrow gangways where *Oma* pulls a hand cart
filled with schnitzel, blintzes, and kraut. Maybe, if I'm lucky
with a red rag tongue hung outta my back pocket
on October's first cool night. The sky, another oil puddle rainbow.
Night swelling like a black balloon. Or maybe not.
What else matters, if the odds are the odds?
Tucked inside the crankcase or staring out the L window:
what's always been this way, trying not to be left.

LOOKING BACK AT 21ST AND HOYNE, CHICAGO

Beneath a night incapable of stars,
faith flickers and swoons.

In my hands, gin in a jelly jar.
That was homesickness; this is silence.

From a cardinal sky,
the rain's uneasy percussion plays against my roof,

another former school.
The Pink Line train jostles and jolts through Pilsen.

How one promise breaks another
is what remains important.

Facing an uncertain sadness
through a soft scoop of apricot.

Forgetting you becomes *rebuilding me*.
At Paulina, graff writers paint murals

and moms hold their children like paper people chains.
I never belonged, but I wanted to.

What's the point of November on an empty street?
A winter sky, leaves whishing, a voice quaking.

My mother's music books in the piano bench seemed enormous.
I remember her sketching raccoons.

Later, I bought cherries from a pickup truck.
You are gone, but also you've been gone.

To absolve into a bright forgiveness.
I wonder how the gratitude will shake out.

Is this happy?
Or is this doubt licking the brim?

I think I know.
Though it should be no surprise that I am always looking out

when the sun dips low.
In this way, I've learned to focus

on what's here and what's not,
as in this still night emptied of stars, filled-in blue.

Three...

"Lullaby" by Esteban del Valle

IN MY LITTLE BOOK OF THINGS I WRITE DOWN

—for and after Mary Ann Samyn

Here's a toaster. Here's a dress.
The ribbon I think matters.
Let's begin here.
This is a question for you, but the rest of you can answer in your hearts.
So much bullshit happens in a day, don't you think?
There's a '70s song for everything.
You tell us a lot, but not everything.
Shame is good. You can work with that.
You just need to give up a little bit. Giving up is useful sometimes.
I don't like parakeets.
Denny's is a powerful place.
You don't want to announce honesty. You just do it.
Don't settle. Dreams are tough.
Praying is fine. Maybe forgiveness is right.
You can own that word if you want. Pull it behind you in a little wagon.
And it really turns out you haven't been loved enough.
Sometimes half-sorry is as sorry as you can be.
All of which is to say,
Honey, put that pillow down. Put that dirty pillow down.
Shame is a theme tonight.
I don't think I'd like to know about hydroponics.
I don't really care for modern life.
I think little kids are good at burial. They're low to the ground already.
How is that possible?
Pigs agree to do a lot of strange things.
Is there a classy karaoke? It could happen in winter, I feel.
What's the regret here?
A useful mystery.
Your material will run out and then the only thing you'll have left
is what the rest of us have: a sunny day.

WHEN YOU SAID THAT, I NEVER SAID THIS

That walk from the library to your car,
the night pregnant with silence.
Unable to speak because it was an ending.
So all we did was breathe.
Walk and breathe. Until in the parking lot,
two bright pink crab apples,
their blossoms carved out of night.
One bloomed upright,
the other drooped like low-hung fruit.
I don't know what this is.
It's not the April I know.

WE DO WHAT WE DO

I can't find north in West Virginia.
Beneath the pine-shade on Lillian,

I've run the way I've always run;
the way anger borders love.

How the spoon bends a certain way.
Maybe I'll never know what's right.

Beneath a streetlight, a star trail.
Sometimes silent is as loud as I can be.

I'D RATHER NOT SAY

I only see you when you hide
inside the low rumble of a thousand bees.
And to think that yesterday I held you
between the lemon-sting of a hangnail,
and the night stepping out from behind October
that called you into its dark cloud.
I watched you leave
and stain the sidewalk with a velvet gloom.
The wind blew through the pines
and the muscle between my ribs grew cold.
You said you hated how dead leaves filled your ears
with smoke and moon. I wrapped my lips
around the mouth of a wine jug
and drank to the last drop. And when I woke,
you were still disappearing between particles of light.
And the black drag of memory
scraped out my insides with its cold spoon.

THE IRRATIONALITY OF ANGER

Sometimes I feel like the god of missteps,
walking along the perimeter of last night's hazy memory,
screaming at someone I love
in a way that suggests that I don't.

You said, *Ten hours from now*
this will all be a distant memory of pain.
A week has flown by
and the grackles are still gathered on my shoulders.
I know what I deserve.
And I know what you don't.

Nothing is working
and my threadbare memory
is flecked with my foolish desire to fight.
The only thing tossed around now
is the shame I've forced upon you,
which has swelled in me, now that I'm sober.

Let me tell you something
about rampant pilfering of the heart.
Beneath a dry knoll of pinched breath
the dialogue of our unsaid movie plays
and a cloud of bees
flies from my open mouth.

THIS IS WEST VIRGINIA, NOT LOS ANGELES, AND ALL OF A SUDDEN I FEEL OLD

From the porch decking board, your window aglow
and some nights I wondered
for who.

All the sadness of homes forgotten
in the great blocks of quiet.

In the mind, bright July; or at least, I'm *trying*.
Between the moments, feeling loved and unloved.

The soft squeeze of the floor beneath, a loud creak.
What small comfort grows in my quiet tide of worry?

The muddy river, Phil's passing;
the fatal motorcycle crash of a local poet,
the leather-topped desk I sold him.
In all directions, a bitter song.

All the wolves in the world. On my lip,
my tongue: *the unsaid window.*

Today's panic attack is a hole
torn out of a wall in a doctor's office.

Maybe it's never too late to say I'm sorry;
or maybe I'm only sorry because you're not.

FEELING OUT OF PLACE AT HOME

Where I monitor what my father eats,
where the corporate cubicle's minor regrets
reflect off Lake Michigan like dim stars.
The sunset bleeds toward another planet
while sailboats bob on the water.
The sky is cloudy; our future cloudy.
But let's shoot the barrel rim,
hammer weathervanes, wake up happy
from this dream where we're falling
between the gaps in the leaves;
between the branches, we stay.
Let's get twisted like cocktails
between the sheets of the afternoon,
tattoo sunflowers inside our dreams.
It's summer again, and I'm kayaking
with my father, unsure if I want kids,
but on the lake the dusk is lovely.
I feel lost between clouds and their reflection,
here at home, hoping the song's final note
echoes inside someone long after I'm gone.

AFTER GRAFFITI, NORTHSIDE CARBONDALE

I'd like to say: the grief is gone and there's room for more.
But the loud knock of railway coupling
opens starlight over this small Midwestern town
where shiny black railroad tracks bore through
me, grappling and collapsing under a question:
what pearls did the stranger give you? Your face,
a gloomy love note. The word *timing* heavy in my ear;
the weight of never. A common nightmare. This is
some day I'll love myself. See the breaks in the leaves.
Here, where the buds are green and regrets' blossom is cotton white,
hope will get you in trouble. What fades into the long quiet
is sunlight becoming therapy. I wonder.
Meanwhile, the crack between *what if* and *letting go* heals,
scarves of snow blow down ruts in the freight yard.
From where I sit, through an open window,
a salty breeze moves inward, once, then once more.
The scent of wet barley and gravel carries me
to Illinois in October, a fondness there,
a teenaged needling, until sad words chisel through,
What do you want from me? What I need
is to be back on the rails again, painting my name on rusty metal;
rodent bones crackling beneath my shoes. In exchange
for a still-wet stamp on a grainer, aerosol fumes rising
through elm, ash, and sycamore. My hoodie up,
burning leaves trapped in the fabric, where you are with me.
Fingers paint-stained harbor blue.
As I step from the train yard, a horn blasts in the North.
I'm afraid of being nobody. I want the clouds to know my name.

THERE'S ALWAYS SOMEONE LEAVING

Beneath the watery twilight,
it's my last summer in West Virginia.
How difficult it is to forgive
someone for what they didn't do.
Now, the river is green.
Somehow this speaks to me.
When I was born, could I taste the bruise
growing inside my mother?
How she drank in the early years
turned into how I drink now,
alone and full of something akin to longing,
because love has a way of going missing.
And what can we do, but sniff each rose
or grow jealous from a stranger's laughter?
It's May now. The leaves are spring-green.
The grass is after-the-rain-green.
The storm clouds, a green-blue.
What is it inside me that needs to leave
these people who seem to love me?

THE PERFECT TIME TO LEAVE ONE HOME FOR ANOTHER

After the grill smoke eases from the alleys and tears into tufts of cloud.
After the moving trucks are packed with taped-up boxes,
and the roll-down doors are slammed closed.
After the final gold-and-blue firework pops and crackles.
After *I love you* quiets and you find someone new,
I'll be in Montana. Maybe in Kalispell. Maybe Glacier.
Maybe home in Silver Bow, but I'll think of you here.
I'll worry and remember and try to focus on what's good.
How the chimney carves its blocky silhouette
out of the end of May, a purpling-pink sunset. I'll remember
instead of how I often forget. Among the pastel light
that darkens, beneath the streetlamp that flickers and glows
outside this lonely room, in this lonely town,
the one you've been in for so many years now.
But this isn't home, is it? And it never will be.

THE PRACTICE OF BECOMING ONESELF

I think about guilt, at twenty-three, watching you bang
on our dealer's windows at 4 AM because the baggie ran out.
And how, who I've become—a Writing Instructor, a Cedar Lake kayaker,
an appreciator of pre-war motorcycles—is crazy different.
How the poignancy of Maggie Anderson
pops like graffiti on fresh brick; Bazooka Joe in my thirties.
How, last night, a supercell gathered over Fort Kern,
a funnel twisting its lid, and I sipped, as I do, with purpose.
How the neighborhood black cat rolled at my feet
until, inside, the stray roamed rooms, trying to find its place.
As do I, although I didn't have those words then.
And how that same cat rushed back out into the drizzle.
Something outside more comfortable than in.
I've felt opposite, living in this world, for as long as I can remember.
Then, I squeeze another lime into another Michelada and drink it down,
watch day turn into night, and call my father.
We talk about me buying a Crosstrek,
Roth IRA's, and the benefits of frequent flyer miles.
We talk this way because soon I'll be in Montana.
And the practical nuances of adulthood are easier to discuss
than love and the absence of one another. But in this way,
of course, that's precisely what we've been talking about all along.

EVERYTHING, ALWAYS

Let's define the question. Purple Canterbury bells in the yard
and Millie sniffing bushels of baby's breath from Rocker to Grizzly Trail;
ten thousand miles of mining tunnels beneath her paws,
and the Northern Rockies tinted blue by the waning western light.
Why is it so hard to enjoy things?
Maybe tomorrow will be better; though I've been alone most of my life.
Later, in the flats, by Pete's Antler Art or the RV Park,
I think of Gonzo's and Hong Kong Harry's fireworks' stand,
rolling down Kaw Avenue, searching for something—
end tables, abandoned railways, happiness.
With the sun warming what's left,
I head for Platinum, the park on Mercury, then home.
But I'll never forget what it's like
when I'm in the spot I want to be in most.
Maybe the problem is we're always searching
to feel good not knowing. But you can erase anything:
pink helicopter seeds dusting the underside of a maple,
the rusty-rose underbelly of a cloud moving north,
and feeling robbed of your past. Maybe is better than no.
So, what's the calculus? Why any of this?
The story you come with isn't the one you leave with.
We're not dead and there's still hope.
Make some time to listen, before it's too late.

PURPLE TONIGHT, I GUESS

Walking Montana's Copperway,
Anselmo's headframe
looms like a body
porch-watching evening
darkening Tabletop Mountain.

Lupine clover, sagebrush,
and lady's bedding sprouts
from craggy dust.
Barbed-wire-choked gardens
and middle-class Victorian mansions

climb Uptown
to the unpretentious bungalows
in Walkerville, where rust-red Ford trucks
rest on blocks
or with bricks jammed under tires.

How strange that rap music
now drums the tin roofs
on Caledonia Street, where the words
of a miner who walked from Detroit
to Butte remain.

But I'm the stranger now,
another one who walks
to the playground
on Mercury
where the swing sets are still.

But before this
I watched my father
watch his wife,
my mother, walk into rehab
for the first time.

It was about her,
but now it's not.
That's enactment;
don't we all know
to celebrate silence,

the great silence?
Another thing is:
we got somewhere;
it's just not
where we wanted to go.

We've all witnessed
the monster isn't a monster,
paint-chipped porches,
and *I can live with that.*
Yesterday,

I read about Desperation,
that's the fan tower
where Pigeons congregate,
where warm air breathes
out of Anselmo

which it served,
and afterwards I saw a mother
folding children's clothes
in an RV, and I wondered,
where have you been?

But I also saw
Queen Ann's Lace
and tall grass
poke between the rocks
and later in my kitchen

I bit a cherry
and let it bleed
between my lips,
spit the seed,
and practiced forgetting.

How funny when I say it:
it all makes sense.
The way pills taste
when chewed
is the way blood tastes too.

So, what's the takeaway?
You hope
for something better.
You can't be certain either.
That's a kind of healing.

A PRETTY GOOD FOR NOW

Storm clouds blocked
by the eastern ridgeline
explode and billow
into new forms of self.
So, what is it you want?
I'm tired of pretending
it's need. The tulips'
green leaves sprouted—
the bulbs didn't make it.
But that's Butte,
that's what they say.

EVERYTHING'S INCREDIBLE AT THIS POINT

—after Emily Berry

At night in Montana I forget who you are
My memory could change
How can I stop my memory from changing
Pink bands of light stretch over the Rockies each morning, so this is mourning
I don't know what your fears are
You say I'm the only one who knows you
But all I know are my fears
Are your secrets
They're spruce branches creaking in the canyon
I don't expect another like you
This conviction kept me up all night, like geese thumping into walls
At dark; or snow blown over a gray road like loose chalk
I'm not looking for perfection
Glass bits glint beneath the low-white moon
Until Butte glows with halos of amber light
One never knows how much of the journey will be alone
I just want to get there in a different way
Through the eye of a camera
Tell me what kind of life you want
This is me guessing
There must be no capacity for hope

FIRST MONTANA, NEXT WYOMING

I reconsider things.
In this series of matte-blue mountains,
it's all so fraught. Broken Arrow Steakhouse
and Casino, Craft Beer exit 187,
Dead Horse Creek Road.
What was it you said about the moon?
Two cows on a haybale and a fan tower
stuck like a straw deep in the mountain—
blowing air in, sucking air out.
What it must be like to breathe so easy.
A bright yellow bird above the windshield.
I suppose you could say, I wanted a little problem;
but there were only silver streams
running through spokes of wagon wheels
and aspen trees with trembling green leaves
and a gold Chevelle with the trunk popped in a pasture,
red rock highways, Bighorn Mountains—
an elephant row powdered with snow.
Leaving anywhere can be beautiful
and it's not just the antelopes
and mustangs running alongside the car.
It's saying *fine* to not knowing
what it's like for love
to be the ending.

ACKNOWLEDGMENTS

I gratefully acknowledge the editors and readers of the following journals in which these poems or earlier versions appeared.

Appalachian Heritage: "Summertime Chi";
Barely South Review: "Illinois Breakdown";
Barrow Street: "In My Little Book of Things I Write Down" and "We Do What We Do";
Bayou Magazine: "What Remains";
Chicago Quarterly Review: "Feeling out of Place at Home";
Cimarron Review: "The Good Life";
The Fourth River: "Morning in West Virginia";
Gulf Stream: "The Practice of Becoming Oneself";
Hawai'i Pacific Review: "Sixth Grade Autobiography";
Hot Metal Bridge: "After Graffiti, Northside Carbondale";
Kestrel: "We Don't Take Breaks, We Just Break";
The Meadow: "First Montana, Next Wyoming";
the minnesota review: "The View from Here";
Muzzle Magazine: "Hepburn Manor, Los Angeles";
Nashville Review: "All That Matters";
Ninth Letter: "Just Once";
Pembroke Magazine: "The Irrationality of Anger";
Permafrost: "After You Almost Divorced Your Husband";
Poet Lore: "The Perfect Time to Leave One Home for Another";
Salt Hill: "It Always Does";
San Pedro River Review: "Apple Orchard Road";
The Sewanee Review: "The Perfect Time to Walk Out of Someone's Life";
Sierra Nevada Review: "Boulder, Colorado, 1989" and "This Is West Virginia, Not Los Angeles, and All of a Sudden I Feel Old";
The Southampton Review: "How the Journey Worked";
Sugar House Review: "I'd Rather Not Say";
Third Coast: "Concessions";
Yemassee: "Yeah, Sure," and "We're Not There Yet";
Zone 3: "Looking Back at 21st and Hoyne, Chicago."

"Explain Yourself" was selected by Kevin Stein for the Gwendolyn Brooks Poetry Award (3rd place) in the Illinois Emerging Writers Competition.

"Thank You, Forgiveness" was selected by Natalie Diaz for the *2017 Best New Poets* anthology.

"Morning in West Virginia" was selected for the *2019 New Poetry from the Midwest* anthology.

"Concessions" was selected for the 2021 issue of *So It Goes: The Literary Journal of the Kurt Vonnegut Museum and Library*.

A recording of "Hepburn Manor, Los Angeles" was a finalist for the *Missouri Review* Audio Prize and was featured on their podcast.

"In My Little Book of Things I Write Down" is composed entirely of Mary Ann Samyn's comments during graduate poetry workshops from Spring 2016 – Fall 2017 at WVU.

Thank you to West Virginia University's MFA program, Montana Tech, and Butler University for your generous support.

Thank you to all my professors and friends. You know who you are.

Big thanks to Esteban del Valle for granting permission to use his artwork on the cover and for the chapter breaks.

Thanks to Maggie Anderson for the endorsement. It's an honor to have your words on the book jacket.

Endless thanks to Mary Ann Samyn. This would've never been possible without your friendship, mentorship, and guidance.

A special thanks to David Dodd Lee. I'm grateful to you for believing in this one and for your editorial leadership. You made this manuscript into a book and put it into the hands of readers. I can't thank you enough—truly.

Finally, thank you to my family—the whole sprawling tree.

Bryce Berkowitz is the winner of the Austin Film Festival's AMC TV Pilot Award. His poems have been selected for national and regional anthologies, including *Best New Poets* and *New Poetry from the Midwest*. He is a recipient of the Illinois Emerging Writers | Gwendolyn Brooks Poetry Award and a winner of the *Big Muddy* | Southeastern Missouri State U. Short Story Competition. His writing has appeared in *The Missouri Review*, *The Sewanee Review*, *Ninth Letter*, and other publications. He teaches at Butler University.